Free Verse Editions

Edited by Jon Thompson

Quarry

Carolyn Guinzio

Parlor Press
West Lafayette, Indiana
www.parlorpress.com

Parlor Press LLC, West Lafayette, Indiana 47906

Printed in the United States of America
S A N: 2 5 4 - 8 8 7 9

Library of Congress Cataloging-in-Publication Data

Guinzio, Carolyn.
 Quarry / Carolyn Guinzio.
    p. cm. -- (Free verse editions)
 ISBN 978-1-60235-085-4 (pbk. : acid-free paper) -- ISBN
    978-1-60235-086-1 (adobe ebook)
 I. Title.

PS3607.U5426Q37 2008
811'.6--dc22
                                        2008041905

Cover art: "Luna" by Anita Huffington; photograph by
    Michael Korol. Used by permission.
Author photo by Warren McCombs. Used by permission
Printed on acid-free paper.

Parlor Press, LLC is an independent publisher of scholarly
and trade titles in print and multimedia formats. This book
is available in paper and Adobe eBook formats from Parlor
Press on the World Wide Web at http://www.parlorpress.
com or through online and brick-and-mortar bookstores.
For submission information or to find out about Parlor Press
publications, write to Parlor Press, 816 Robinson St., West
Lafayette, Indiana, 47906, or e-mail editor@parlorpress.com.

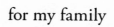
for my family

Contents

Quarry

The Weekend Book

Large Blue

There is a saying that sheep
built our churches, but the eye
cannot record a happening so gradual.
What fossils form as August evenings
drag over the length of the world.

The Large Blue caterpillar is eating
wild thyme. It will fall in Fall
to the ground and be carried
by ants to their hill.
They will keep it alive.

They love its sweet secretion
and feed it even their less precious
young. In the shelter of an anthill
it lives through the winter
that would see it dead.

We may mold the beasts we eat,
but little things nest in the large:
The louse of typhus, the black rat
that took peasants and let land
slip into weedy anarchy.

Weathers

By June, the risk of frost is past, but in May
growers build bonfires around their orchards,
lighting those on the windward side when it
is expected. Lunar haloes, red sunrise, a break
of blue that would make a Dutchman's jacket.
You will find groves of oak and holly
where light has not fallen on the leaf-mould
beneath since Domesday, and in it, an adder
with a belly of porcelain blue. The festival
of ice men, the forty-day deluge of rain
Swithun conjured to keep the monks from moving
his grave. Frost creeps in the branches at night
and blackens the heart of a blossom.

Food & Drink

The names of apples roll around the tongue:
Duke of Devonshire, King o' the Pippins.
The humble Annie Elizabeth, farmer's girl.
It is not for the garden shade or cottage alone
that you will be judged. Tomorrow's duck,
cut up, should simmer in the gravy of today's
stewed hare. If you have a seashore,
seaweed and cloth, oysters and hours
to spare, make a circle of flat stones and a fire.
Lay them in their shells on the blue
bed of ashes. Put the halves of eggs back
together. The aromatic oils of the coffee bean,
the weary walker's counsel of despair.
Sidecar, John Wood, Satan's Whisker.
Keep everything that should be, cold.

Acts of Enclosure

To please his eye, to conceal from a lordling the sight
of other humans living, they started a spinney.
Barrows on its edges mark planter's graves.

The ecology of rich men has much to do with sport:
The fox hunter's large and scattered covert; for grouse,
moors with heather to burn. It's into the best cricket-bat

that these willows will bend. Rivers being less
artificial than land, fishermen work over them:
salmon-ladder, weir, dam, diversion. Cutting the water-

weeds, reedbeds and growth on the bank. They retreat
into walls hewn from the quarries: the bracken,
the furze. Carp bump in a stew-pond dug by Monks.

Common Names & Companies

Present in every garden,
the spug and ruddock,
the ousel and mistle-
thrush. Mavis with her
emotional quality
listens as shufflewings
sing sissi-weeso
in their glistening
bowl: Moss, cobwebs,
feathers and down.
What do we imagine
for the old man, devil-
bird, butcher or storm?
In their companies,
we call them Dopping
and Spring. Murmuration:
Starling. Exaltation:
Lark. A fall of woodcocks
gasps in the dark,
shuffling out of our path.

Of Ancient Lights

Light in the eyes of the law is ancient
after twenty years. The sun must reach
the church arch and transom,
the windows of timber-
built homes. We fixed the divisions

of the calendar: Nothing
should have to be born
more than once. In January:
ploughing— No season is dead.
February stabs at winter with barren

strawberry. We doze on the cold
morning lawn and behead
its sprouted daisies.
The willowherb fluff will be blowing
next month. In clear and root-

lifted October, animals bury
the last hazelnuts. Weekenders
finding fault with the Earth
can look into space for comfort.
Through our framed hands we see:

Mercury with no procession of night,
Venus wrapped in clouds,
Sea of Crises, Sea of Mists,
the starry river splitting.
What can we on Earth still hold

when Autumn ends? Woodsage,
hogweed, prickly and stripped,
like a scarecrow's umbrella of bone.
A tremendous question hangs
in the December sky.

The Language of Flowers

Bramble: Envy; because it hates its neighbors.
Pigeons stand blinking at their red wire feet.
Don't turn your face from me: Gold Thread;
Grape: My two eyes, your right hand and dried
Iris tied at the neck— glittering residue, fingertips, throat.
The swallow leads a double life.

Should you wish to indulge in a private meaning,
If we lie in a vast aggregate of stars,
If you lack both flowers and the power of speech,
spell it— *humble, kind*— in the palm
before bodies of water, light and forest
floor twitching: Leaves and what grows beneath.

The experience of sequences is not the only guide.
Late, the swallow's last clutch left to starve,
One is tempted not to witness; Thistle:
Fearless: One is tempted not to be.
Breath held purple limbs against the fence.
I die, Gold Wire: Come quickly.

Alive Enough

We stood by a pond that winter day,
on the rotting dock, tossing dog food
to the pleading mouths of catfish
as they surged from the water to eat.

We've all heard of the last gathered strength:
Sitting up, widened eyes, words.
The one who sits next to the bed is alone.
The one who is propped on the bed is alone.

On the bowed scraps of hammered wood,
we were unnerved, thrown off
by any movement: Our own, the other's,
connected and discrete. The sky held no

phenomena, no blue-lit planet marked
the moonset. There were no summer
strays left among the birds. The air
was good. If it was better somewhere else,

we didn't think of it. There is no definite
sense, no moment when the last scrap of grief
lifts away. The catfish ate with what seemed
to be pleasure. The water was growing

a cold-weather sheen. The fatter catfish
lolled among the stones, letting little ones clean
the last floating crumbs. It was windless
and bright. It was time to step back on the earth.

Quarry

We leave of ourselves a shelter.
What give has the petrified arm,
outstretched, on which a hunting bird
could rest in stillness for an hour.
Days of little light; bones and rock
are nothing without heat. We will pause
in our work, hat in hand, for the bones,
but against our shouldered machines
it will yield, workable rock of the earth.
The jutting bluffs falling far into the future
land so hard as to sink. While workers
devil the rock in gleaming bins, fires
heat the rusting bins, warming the fists
of the homeless who wait for work,
for shelter, for the old wool blankets
rumored to be thrown from trucks
on hard freeze nights. A geologic face
looks out from the rock and wants
for a body, a spine, inhumanly stretched
into an eave, to leave of itself a shelter.

Medium Reading the Veins in the Wrist

You will hang things made
from trees in the trees, or,
trees made from other things,
ideas of trees. You will
gather and eat the scattered

coal, mica, the hematite
and dolomite. Sparks
of water-washed mineral
crystals still course through
your blood. You will hang

lemon balm upside down
in the corners to soak away
the electric venting of the dead.
But the dead will still dent
the drapes. You will want

not to know things that
you know. The drapes will
draw the eye from the painted
ceiling to the stone-
lined floor. You will hang

them outside in the trees
to let breezes carry away
the dark flecks in their folds.
Like a tooth in the tiniest fiber:
It is. It is in them and in you for good.

Astral

Gutted gray eye, following the headlights of a car.
Who is moving through the darkness, alive? What light pools
through the fall trees, trees still green but beginning?
What moon— hunger, thunder— watches us squander
small days behind blinds: Haze over city, chair propped
under door? The daring jumping spiders carry green moons
on their backs, feeling, in the heat, the greater heat of prey.
They listen for distant events, rising with the wave
of approach before the whine. The blurry
phosphorescence on their backs leaves a wake,
caught in the motion sensor light. Gray gutted eye,
do you know: Where will they fall? Whose wheat
will burn? Where can we lock it away, our breath,
when they land on the flammable earth?

Ivan's First List

On the hook in a locked stall.
Jammed halfway down the pipe.
In deepest stacks, in footnotes.
Ripe for the stealing, in the field.
Where someone would walk a dog.
Among forlorn asparagus on a fence.
Under the trays of a Polish bakery.
You can hear the trains from there.
Digging beneath an uncrossable road.
Asleep on the margin of the road.
Beyond vision, with wounded cats.
In a place between places, the coat
closet under the stairs. Albumen
clinging to the cracked shell.
Thrown around the marble horse.
Prone across a reeking couch.
At the gallery seats in the Hall.
On a stool in the hotel bar.
Soothing the scorched grass.
In the putty that filled the gash.
On the red chin of a vulture.
In the mouth of an ant on a feather.

Order Is the End
of Everything

The lake is shaped
like a hand, five lines
fanned out. The draggers
emerge from their houses
uncalled, somehow

knowing when the nets
are needed, sensing
an abscessed shelter
arising, an absence
expanding within:

To search
for the missing
before they are
missed. Gently
beckoning open palm,

we all would rest
upon it. The gars
and minnows make
our fortunes wily,
make unexpected turns

like water on glass, or bats.
They obey the bugs
and contours we can't see
and will rest on what feels
to them like a bed, while we,

soft-skulled, first felt
our thread-like neck
so cradled, and since
have searched for water
that holds the same heat

as a body. To wade in,
unfeeling. The too-late shouts,
the shore, are stars receding.
Turned over, to cover,
the lake is an upturned cup.

Crossing

Standing in pairs in the yard, eight deer
guard over their own fly-torn skin.
The round surface is tipping out of view,
sweet leaves, roses with oil worth the risk
of a spike in the tongue are pulled over
the horizon with a patience that the deer
don't know. They reach with necks
and teeth, the large and darting eyes
that even thieves let slump once the stolen
things are gotten home. In their cells,
they know the sound of someone watching,
the taste of the tops of trees, the unbreaking
wire-thin bones of the leg, bent in the middle
to run. Matching as they do the tired, winter
trunks in woods, you could be leaning on one
suddenly, betrayed at the last second
by a gasp and wrenching. There is nothing
but a scattering of feathers on the floor
to connect us. Our blood quickening in us,
we look out at the thing that we fear.

Spare

I

Slivers of white dishes on a wood floor.
White cows in drought-dead fields.
Being dusted, swept away.
Slack nerves make for dropped dishes.
A bus stopped at the edge of a field.
Being dusted; given dust,
made up of what makes the nerves go slack.
Descending the steps of the bus
at the wrong but appointed time.
They know the local words for weeds
and birds. Little world, hard to leave.
The stack of white china was empty and clean.
It was unfinished. It had not yet begun.

II

We are all breathing the same thing,
our eyes turned away, our lungs
buried out of view. Together
on the train, we are contained,
speeding through the fine space
between clear and silver, pouring
back out of the holes we drilled
in the earth. Ar article is stuck,
sucked to the grate, quelling the question.
At the stops, we are all watching
the blurs slur down to letters,
streets named for reasons
long ago razed, the shapes,
crops, and daughters fading
shades under the grid.

III

Dust rises with our every move,
then falls. The bus, green, silver,
white, on a road through the rows
of crops. In the space between
where the bus ends and the train
begins, five thousand small hearts
are slow in the fat-fronted
dickcissel finches, dying from eating
one round of seed, given up to save
the remainder. The girl in her one
good dress sleeps standing up.
The crops will arrive cleanly wrapped,
no trace of a former story.

IV

Wrap the shards in heavy cloth.
They will work into the skin.
We could breathe glass.
They say *rain dove, sparrow hawk.*
They say *buzzard*:
spoken things, breathing things, unfixed.
In the book, a kestrel watches a field,
white in the empty margin.
The girl, below the slack strung wire,
waits by the sign, looks up
from her guide to see
an almost weightless thing
jump to hover nine feet from earth,
waiting for the perfect
second to connect.

Weather Curve

Iridescent flies are writhing on the driveway.
We set up our chairs to watch, while the crows,
in uneasy groups of three, keep up their low-throated
mutterings in the cedar. Who hasn't reached a point
when they don't care who's watching, and aired
the open folds? The system is swinging north.

It will miss us, sprinkling only a spell of restless
sleep, our minds not free of the idea of it: People
are standing on the land by the lake, shouting
to the people in their boats in the lake about what
they can't see behind them. The children ask why
the ride home seems shorter. The unexpected, too,

unfolds slowly. Who hasn't missed what they weren't
looking for, and petted the Black Widow's eggs
tacked up to the underside of a chair? Falling faces,
such things have been creeping up on you.
The system is red in the center, undulating in and out
of an oval as the animation tracks it north. Men keep

their collections in the basement, in the lower-level
sheds, the ever-dank relegations most prone to flood.
So taken are they with anger and love, the crows skip
their ritual proclamations on being spared the storm.
The driveway flies are spent and they blink, dissolving
the mist into the salty southern edges of their eyes.

Wave Archive

Once there was a wave, small and clear,
when the earth tipped the waters of the great
lake west to the beer-glass-scattered edges.
It took a toy car with no wheels when it left,
out to the upper reaches. The water was closed
for swimming. We walked toward each other
to meet at a spot you could see from the sky,
the satellite tugging its leash. Here, the lake keeps
the unrepeatable, randomly giving back
what was gone. The holes in the sand
where the ants burrow, the car in the glass:
They were there all along. We risk reaching in
to the wrist, to the east, to the hour ahead.

A Sense of It

I have bad news. We arrived together. We walked
down the long hallway and out of the basement and
under the fluorescent-paneled ceiling. You were talk-
ing about being a child. You knew a full day before
the rain would arrive, by the smell the air carried.
You knew a full hour before the train would arrive,
and who it carried. When you were a child, everyone
thought there were two kinds of days: a normal day
and a bad day. They desired a bad day so the tedium
of a normal day would again be desirable. As soon as
a bad day became more desirable than a normal day,
you could see it in the way they looked at you. You
used to think, how easy it would be to make them this
gift. Maybe it happened that way. We left together,
walking up the stairs and out of the basement where
the ceiling was covered with fluorescent panels. You
were talking about the news. You said, I climbed the
tower, to better see what was coming. The street was
full before us. You said, I have bad news.

Seen from One Angle

The plastic sapphires broke
from their thread
and landed in the grass.
City dwellers feel a muted
sense of movement

in the sky, bump and give
on shower nights, the meteors
streaking unseen among
the artificial beams.
Still, the sky imposes

a low static crackle,
a murmur of distant events.
When the lights we can see
in the dark recede,
the dark things that catch

the light will send
their tiny blinding beams
to the black eyes of crows.
They will come with a prehistoric
lurch, a predatory

swagger and care.
Delicately and with strange
delight, they will pluck up
secret, sparkling things
that only they can see.

Counting

The birders lie dressed in their beds,
gravely waiting. Soon, they will step
out in the dark with their pages of lists
and boxes. Have seen, Have seen:
They will mark them off. Their quarry
is one of two shrikes in the county: Butcher
birds spearing their weight in elephant
stag beetles on barbed wire. Louder
human power will ignite the place you live.
Remember the mounted head of the pig
on the fence, facing away from the soon-to-be-
burning house. The shrike is not a mocking
bird, though gray with white wing patches.
Have not seen, empty box, and yet it is,
still is. The birders will fill their boxes
and wait to see what change it brings.
The things that they will see and miss
this morning will be there, the round moon
a small piece in the great funnel leading to the eye,
the lens of the field glasses even wider than
the moon. The beak of the shrike, bearing a beetle,
will only take shape as the moon dissipates.

Bent Trillium

Blood & Paint

Consonant sky, cut by white,
            the oval
is always covered.

On a low chair, mixing color, a painter
            will not pin
the living in place.

Hold
            (in every lot, a thicket)
still for me.

Let me hold the thorns aside.
            They grow here
for you, they spring back

as if it never rained.

A wild ivory and burgundy,
            an open center
sleeping.

Have you ever been
            moonless, a sound
follower?

A painter will let
        each of three leaves
arrow the lines between

her fingers, the edges
        against
each other, a falling

gradual, so much so
        you may not
know.

Flood Plain

Water skimmers knock
against the grass,
the pull of our shoes.

In her words:
> I was not so unloved
> in the world, not so
> without reciprocity,

> not easy

> to say it was my own
> bones I wanted
> to hold against the sky.

Filled treads lead
to the lit
spot, the chair.

Night Lot

Storm-angled thistle and chicory sprout
Around rails. Trains river you out of a city.
In dark, switch light bleeds
Into the fields, or green corn dark
Is purpling toward the fluorescence.
Beneath her sloping top-story porch,
The criminal and the law call up
From their chase: The comfort of a common
Lot, the ennobling mortal nearness.
Smaller still at the edge of an alley,
A praying mantis drains its green to gray.

Interpreted Walk

In truth, there is no point
from which we can see.
You are in the gloom of standing
timber. The bridge is a bridge of chanting.
(Hold up your palm and say) Listen.
Listen. The things that rolled up
still roll up against us. There is always
one chair at the edge of a river.
What the emptiness means is what
your emptiness means: What is growing?
Is it cold? If I am turned under, will I be
left? Stay close. The mud is wanting.

Three Leaves

You can see that the first
freeze was sudden: Open

mouths blanket the trail,
caught as if in a loud vowel

calling. A sparkling casing
of ice coffins the half-formed

bloom. The leaf spines
are the last to break down.

The bent back path will heal
itself at thaw. Lined with stones,

the leaves will grow over
the stones. You can't hold

a child on each side anymore.
Is what you see alone still there?

Unmoved, each thing within
has changed, or does it disappear?

Chanting Bridge

The bed beneath is quiet
other than in flood, but above,
a close dissonance, body
leaning on body, the chord
binding us down out of sky.
Nodding under leaves,
the weight of thought
draws down the eye: There,
in the story, the hopper
and the wasp. Put your palms
to your ears and listen. Listen.
It narrows. It allows
only one note at a time.

Filled Treads

They carry you away, beside the empty chair.
Half-sunk in river mud, what the emptiness means.
If you are turned under, it doesn't disappear.
These are replicas of the original: shoes, flowers, chair.
She knew the bed, the water, the body can't be caught.
Mixing color, a painter, a child on each side.
Steady yourself on yourself and look down. Look down.
Your prints are replicas of the original prints.
Our treads will carry them away, the seeds.
What sprouts in the alley, an edge of the lot.
The rails, the river, everything, wearing it down.

Moonless

Where there is nothing, a sliver will begin.
Where they are walking, voiceless, unquiet,
discord. All the smaller lights are brightened.
Orient yourself and think, see? See? Useless
for marking the path. Whatever slithers
from their shuffling, shock-breath
drowned in the sound of sumac and weeds
circling their ankles and letting them go.
They walk in the direction of the edge.

Bent Trillium

Stop what you're doing and look.
Look up. What do you not want
to see? The thing has been built

on a single image. Floating
in the water, caught on a worn
stone. A tanager stands on the edge

of the chair. A hopper in the shadow
of a shoe. Missing color, a painter
lifts the bent head, the covered

center, the ivory weather-spread.
A frost is waiting half way around
to change each thing within.

Break them down beneath the cast,
or do they disappear? If it never
rained, the bridge would be useless.

Swimming in the little pools
of her prints, the seeds will carry
down. Down where the root

narrows to allow the thin
drone, a vein. She wanted
to hold her own bones to the sky.

Then, on each side a child still rolled
against us. Now, you have to rise
and raise your eyes.

Of Portrait, of Self

No, never, with one
shoulder raised, did she
try to be still and not
swat flies, webs
drawn over the shoulder,
all hope of rebuilding

not yet abandoned.
To be still and yet
crawled upon, hair
in a pretty twist.
Who looks at what
or who when the brush

is raised, that hesitation
that may not kill, may
not make immortal.
Green, translucent
spider baby, its venom
small but strong.

She pictured herself
answering the door,
framed in space,
not the spiraling vortex
of thumbprints in clay,
among the wheels and sea

sponges lining the stained
and bowing shelves.
In flowing robes,
translucent, her smallness
seen within, her near
disappearance pulled back

from the edge
to the center of the frame,
held still long enough
to be immortally smooth,
contours and scarves,
poised for the punctures ahead.

Not Fever, Not Dream

It began the way it always did: with division.
Stars wash out of the lines she believed,
ripping sheets in a clear but infindable pain.
Her mirror becoming river, she becomes
her daughter, and daughter's ache slips over their eyes.
Constellations unshaped behind it, a storm obscures,
makes drapes of explanation. It was in this light
when the car knifed the brush, a balm of sage and rain
sticking to skin the way it always did.
Nothing invented can match
what senses together invent
when something breaks that shouldn't—
Cells and it's felt over country.
She ran her own hands under water to cool
a child's burn: *I've been where you most fear to be.*

Convalescence

What does a dissipating
sickness leave behind?
First, an outline. Inside,
a fat blankness. Cells
collecting with a numb
layer between them

and the world. Remember
it? There is a defined
tree line against
a definite sky. You like
the place where it dips,
allowing you to watch

the helicopters landing.
There are sounds
that don't come like knives,
even the audible gasps
of the guinea fowl clicking
on like a siren each time

you open the door.
The breezes pushed here
to the landlocked center
from the hurricanes
that decorate the edges
won't make your skin

rise and burn in fear
now. Breath-channeled
voice of the living, tell us,
as soon as you are able
to speak, of the kind
you've been living among.

Ondata

These are the particulars it offers at its height:
One man sat on the dingy and trash-strewn
stretch of lake every day for four months,
driving up in a red Ford Taurus at ten,
getting out with a radio and towel,

an enterprise borne of resentment for not
having done it before. He dares us to notice
the cheap transistor, the reddening
of everything. Just stare straight out
at the water. To the right rise the steel mills

of Gary. To the left, the city, with its mix
of supple curves, young buildings slithering
in the midst of the stiff misery of the old.
Stare straight out on a volatile day,
and forget what edge you're standing upon.

Watering

Salt is all that is left of the water, dull crystals
clinging to the edges of the concrete pot
where angels in relief raise their graceful
robes around the citrus. Barren, its rain-
water leaves softened where we rubbed
the bitter scent onto our hands, into
our singular human grooves. If it, the plant,
has written in its roots a line upon which
it continues, if somewhere in the lining
of the stems the current of an underwatered
relative makes its leaves gleam with the zeal
of anger or revenge, this potency is lost
on us. We kill the bell pepper-shaped leaves
of the sumac again and again as it chokes
the trunk of an osage orange, but we never think
of it rising against us to take back its land.
Squirrels eat the oranges and leave a black
scattering rot in the grass. They lick the minerals
from the edge of the pot, salting their living
water, and taking on the shape of the contained.

Postcards from Renovation, in Order of Arrival

(Tuesday)

First, say: *Today will not end*
as if it never began. Thunderheads are not
gathering. Weary, dolorous girls approach
the doors in pairs. They turn from the calendar
but keep time. I set my watch by them.
I went to yesterday's festival, but no one
was there. I thought I heard music,
but it was only the pudding stones
sliding down the hill. Something ransacked
the yard overnight. The anger, maybe,
at finding everything so dry. There is
nothing to do against that.

(Sunday)

At the Future Home of the New Church, phoebes
caught paper wasps on the wing all afternoon,
their buzzing cut in the throat.
The old church burned. Bad wires or snapped
road lights made the dark darker here,
where they say if you saw someone walking,
you didn't see anything.

(Wednesday)

We're too close too see it.
The eye is a round knot
in the wood pressed against
the grain. Have you ever
held your eye that close
to another eye? Looking
through nothing, we have
to imagine the windows
and walls. Rectangles shape
our sense of things. Any chaos
wrought in the view will end
when it reaches the frame.

(Thursday)

All structure gone around it, the stone
chimney stands. Odd spots for daffodil
patches might mean an old house place,
and here, though the scent from the scorch
marks is cold, you can see, by the rocks,
where the bodies ended. Since then,
the ground has become just another
unbroken thing: Every year, the bulbs
recede, alive under the frozen dirt.

(Monday)

When are you open?
I needed to see you,
but you weren't here.
There was no sign.
The gate was bolted.
Someone passing
told me they heard
you're not well.
What do you have?
Do you own
this place? Do you
own what you have?
Have they found out?
I have something
I need to be rid of.
I need to speak
to the owner.

(Saturday)

We dropped a cross beam
across the creek bottom.
It stops up a glut of dead
leaves. When it was part
of the wide-walled structure,
it gave strength to our aggregate
voices, our constellation.
One of many. Who would sing
outside, into the skinny air,
without a concrete ending,
nothing to cement us to the many?
The walls accepted the deep
and tremulous extremes. The walls
threw them back as a mass.

(Friday)

They tell you
that when you think
you can breathe,
you'll bury
what you draw.
Most trouble starts
near home,
they say,
where you think
you can breathe.
Talk to nine people
and you will hear nine
signs of a change
in the weather:
harbingers,
signals, the breaks,
good or bad,
that will follow.
They all say
the last house
standing after
the twister
will later be taken
by something
from within.

Bolt

Once struck, one will
flinch when the hand
moves. In the corners
of their eyes, gold-
finches see small changes
we can't. Feeding alone
at the seed. Sometimes
even open places seem
to be draped, hung
with pain, a heavy
airless fabric woven close,
pulling down what rod
exists to hold it.
Yet we walk through
as if this could
not be: Talking, talking
about where things landed
after a storm, about
how where they landed
still they lay: Limbs
so near the source
that they are green,
or not yet green,
but as they were
before this. We see
where we may lay
a foundation, but in
what shape, to what
end is yet unknown.

Of all the minutes,
full, dark, and round,
wearing down any thing
once strong, we each
are given one. Once
struck, one stands again,
leaning on the lone
tree in the field,
where a hawk watches
for wind, or life,
or movement, then, that
time should stop, there
in the flattened grass.

Gait

It's our turn to walk on the surface of earth,
packed pockets trampled by ages of faithful,
firm steps of believers in ground. Water finds
a way in a way air doesn't. There can be life
without thought. What we place on the grave
was never living, was pressed through a stencil,
clamping flowers and letters together. Such rain
it would take to make this remembrance dissolve.
It's our turn to walk on the flat, back-hoed earth,
as if air never will drive cracks into pockets, never
bring into being an abyss that will travel like sparks
on a wire to the brain, no embolismic doubt
will bloom into a beautiful network of faults,
invisible under the surface of earth where we walk.

In September

In September, the night
swimmers emerge from
the lake, first walking,
then tossed with a bone-
settling thud. From here,
we can see the round end

of the world and feel
a shudder sent up through
the ground from some
unknowable source.
In September, what unlocks
the lungs, adding to a fore-

boding, picking-up wind.
We step from the eye
and abide by the rules
of this strange sphere:
Dying marks a beginning.
In September, the turtles

try crossing the roads,
and the airports are full
of slow, vacant amblers,
both like orange construction
cones among impatient
swervers. They want a freeze

to kill the dying, to end
the stench of great beetles
upturned in the gutters.
In September, the stones
collect wet marks from leaves:
A heart, a hand, a maple key.

The impression of leaf is left
to cast over the letters
on the stones, while the dead
leaf, the real leaf,
is glued, intact, to the leaf-
shaped lines of a book.

Treefrog in Moonvine

And in the perfect silence
there was sound.
Horn worms marred
the heart-shaped leaves
with holes. A praying

mantis bobbed
on the stem while moths
bore into the blooms,
leaving behind only
the unnoticeable curve

of a wing. Secrecy,
even, emits a low sound.
No one knows
about the crawlspace,
the hollow-bottomed

rocks along the trail,
the places we wait
until everything
is quiet, or everything
that matters to us.

Portico

This is for an easy
indecision, a mercy

from the glare
that drives into the eyes

we were born with,
placed on the front

of the head, the calm
and muscle of the hungry,

watching for the watchful
side-eyes of prey.

Out here stands the animal,
muddying the cracks,

looking out from ledges:
A stark collection of parts.

It is wanting for paper
to be put together

with the same
seamlessness with which

we know ourselves.
What is it to walk

through a door?
Posts cast long oblong

places of shade,
built, in the heat,

for hesitation. There are
only two worlds,

and you cannot remain
in between.

Report

Sentry

One lit lantern rolls down off the roof.
On warm nights, the boys peel up the shingles,
steady their frames against the angles
and watch over other roofs.
Which way are the sirens heading?
What if they are coming here?
Can the groove that holds
the Little Calumet contain all the rain
that keeps falling? Tonight, in a driveway,
the couple that fights is fighting one last time.
Next time will be quiet: *We love. Is that enough?*
No. No. We love is not enough. Now, though,
their late voices carry. Shocked at the shower of sparks,
they jerk their faces to the sky, the breathing,
the smoke and weather alarm. They reach,
but whatever was coming is gone.

Scenario

You didn't know you were missing. You never noticed flyers.
You closed the door to your house. You listened to the weather.
You waited out the warnings. Warm days began with the sound
of robins and ended with the sound of robins. Cracks in the glass
grew in the cold. Blankets covered the legs of the children.
The blinds pulled up at a slant. A book was marked on the table.
An ice storm split the mulberry tree. The gutters, the grass.
One year the rain made a stain on the ceiling. You stood
on a ladder to make the repairs. All along, you were there,
in one of the houses, fixing the house where you lived.

Alternate Endings

Let's say he didn't drop from a height.
Certificate of blank spaces: Unknown.
He left on time, ahead of a rain, the maps
red and certain, not true to the ungiving ground.

He was paying in cash, his hands wrapped
in bandages, a renter, asleep beneath the bed.
Yet slow in our trucks in the blocks
of the cities, we dragged our eyes over strays.

One began with a fist through a window,
a figure retreating on the other side.
One unbroken fall widens the shatter
to a great radius, one disappearance

to a hollowing out. In one, let's say the storm
didn't weaken. Certificate of flattened tree.
He turned, making half-circles in the mud,
and ducked back under the frame.

Semaphore

Someone took a screwdriver and jammed it through the bulbs.
They hammered the bell. But if you stand close in a lull in the trucks,
if a packed heart is not floating down to the Center, if it's windless,
clear, if the boys that haunt the transom have let their limbs
go slack, if the boxcars are pinning their rattle with weight,
if the dragonfly is dying in the gullet of a nighthawk, corking its song,
if you're deaf to your own deafening workings, you can nearly hear
the warning: a click of connection, wheel on rail: *a train, a train, a train.*

Gravelblind

In the darkroom, the image unravels like a ribbon.
Misreadings rise up out of the gray. We wait at the strange
destinations of letters. First, a fog. What will rise
out of the fog? Some trees, a hill, a pond. An odd stalk
or egret is made no more still by being contained
in the still. The egret is an unpigmented stalk until you turn
away. A great gray Figure A standing in the center
begins to seem slumped and heavyhearted.
Because we cannot predict anything, a head becomes a hat
on a head. A man is strapped in wooden wings,
shingled wings, body bent against the heaviness
of theory and marrow. A print-like ripple disturbs the center
of the pond. Brackets are marking a space that appears
neither to start nor to end. We cannot predict anything.

Ramble

I made a line of stones across the middle of my field.
My field is met by the old road, the thruway, the bypass.
The bypass provides the best view. Drivers watched me working.
Working on the line of stones for hours every day,
every day I found new forms printed on the rocks.
The rocks are not mine. I collected them at night.
At night I took my scratches, slithering through wires.
Wire fences could be made of thread. Anyone,
anyone stopped by wire fences would be stopped by thread.
Thread tied with bows to half-rotten sticks. If the mind
minds a sign, the body will follow. No trespassers.
Trespassing and laws of air are of no use to me.
To me, we are all in the small space between air and stone,
and stone marks our last air. Rocks in the dark and alone,
alone of the river bottom are the same as out under the sky,
the sky as it holds over a field, be it hammering, blue,
blue going gray, gray going blue or white. Nothing,
nothing between the air and the earth, sky and the field.
The field in death, brown and flat, or high and wet in life,
life in its openness is here: the cars, the sky, the field,
the stones, of a piece. If, in passing, you recognize one,
one of the rocks as your own, I defer to the power of gaps.

Among the Circus Paintings

To fend it off, the daughters
talk as if she were alive,
near but out of hearing.
Her aquamarine flower-
patterned dress, at least,

is clean. They knew
something was wrong
when it was not.
Voices are what begin
to recede. One span

wraps around the next
like a bandage. The sound
of a fountain is rumored
a balm, so they rest
on its edges and smoke.

They talk about how she
prefers the rushing blood
of trucks through highway
veins to water, the never-
ending hum of human life.

Stratus Opacus

I.

The walk through the fen from the house into town
brought us close to living things too large to pass
on the path: Mouth breathing, bug-worried, coarse-
haired four-leggeds, deigning to stand still and watch
us go. Then the bridge, where white rowers in white
grinned and grimaced, rehearsing. Then the chapels:
echo, rehearsing. If one turns their hardest eyes to
the sky, they are there, the black holes into which the
green lawns and teams, the groomers, singers, and
scientists in idle talks with the dead could be pulled
from the center of their long family lines into the
stone dark neck of the sky.

II.

The woman who sits on the ground in front of the
Cultural Center has draped on herself every scrap
except one. She keeps covered the box of kittens. In
the fog, a man missed the step to the station, a hole
in the middle of the country's concrete. Annul is to
say something done never was. One by one, she takes
the kittens on her lap and gives them food. What happens
to weather a city face? There are pages of questions
that have to be signed. The man landed at Club
Car, where they gave him something for pain. Below
ground it was flooding and we all were flushed to the
street. Widows wait for the Sheridan bus with Stop &
Shop totes they'll take back to the chair and window,
a proper distance from which to see it all.

III.

See the repeating clouds. The record was set so many years ago, when the world of record began. The clouds sink low to the earth. We are looking at each other through them. When we were young, we thought we could hold them. Now, we walk through them when they're low to the earth. We thought we could stand behind them to undress. They sink low while most of us sleep. So many days the heat keeps us from walking, standing instead, a haze scrambling what we see of each other, currents running over our skin. We are not thinking of where it will lead. We are not thinking. Once, we were new and we grounded our eyes on other eyes, and heat held us where we were, moved by nothing but our own need.

IV.

Real or imagined: The ravens are eating snow. Early
morning music comes unwanted through the trees.
Nothing is biting in the cold. We can hack back
branches and go anywhere, leaving our abstractions
on the mattress. Have we been here since everything
changed? Remember how windy it was, the trees
cracking? Was the baby with us? Questioning slows
the momentum, they say. We stop at the house that
was built to be abandoned. It never had any heat.
Skunks turn their backs on it. Last time, the baby
played in the sticks, if the baby was with us. To be in
a place where it happens too slowly to see. The ravens
watched the baby feel the ground for heat, if the baby
was with us and the ravens were still living there, be-
fore everything changed. How do you remember it?

V.

Nineteen years ago today, it rained over Lake Michigan. We stood on the dry rocks at the edge, near the harbor, and watched water fall on water. The world is not small, though the wind brought the rain to our faces. A woman in a tied scarf used small gestures to keep the children from slipping into the water. It was getting dark, and to the east, it was darker, where the future was alone in a room near the lit bridge, under the metal and hovering birds, watching the still-glowing screen of the west. People that used to be together have fallen all over the world, shook down from the sky. Did rain, from its distance, fall over us all? No, the lake alone was in it, but we, at least, were not in it together, holding out our arms to feel the end.

The Trespassers

Whether we kill
or deport them,
our angry inmates,
we feel it
a kindness, sparing

the miserable parties
involved each other's
company. Whether they
wandered or slithered
or flew through

the wide thresholds
or the tiniest
gaps in screens
makes no difference.
Swatters and boots,

bowls and poisons.
A panicking skink
bangs into plastic
walls only inches
apart. A still-

flickering wing, blinking
eye or spasm
or the leg
makes us wince
in remembrance of

what we were
and are: open
skin, our skeletons
like trees, but
not so tall.

Symbol Key

The children have unfolded their mats
on the floor, and they wait in the dark,
their vertical eyes on the charts.
Someone is moving around the room
with the quietness of age, the pain. Her hand
flat and up next to her eye, a girl sees her own
bones lengthen, her skin spreading like a spill
to the size of an ache. How old she will be
when they finally wake, knowing what all
the marks mean. On her hand, steam seems
to rise up from a burn where a drop splashed
up from the kettle. Quietness hastens the cure,
she believes. A pause, a stop, a question. How long
she will have to remember what everything means.

Black Oak

It would be better to talk outside, where it's not easy
to hear, no sense of the end of sentences, the grass
not white, unmarked by the black stamp of the dance
steps. We will go unguided, pawing at the shared
boundary. There are fences around the beds to keep us
from reaching our own conclusions. The kingfisher is
pausing in skimming the pond, unnoticed. They are
said never to be sated but are yet said to sleep. None
of us can help it— we turn from the sun. We stood
and you said, from what do we arise? From a stump,
and we miss not the tree but its shade. There is a more
visceral kind of missing, the nearer the bone a loss. We
were walking together back to the house, its mothy
incandescence, through an unnamed emptiness,
through leaf smoke and against the turning weight.
Where is everything we've been given? It would be
better to look inside, where nothing is likely to be.

Dart & Balloon

She brought
the fish
home
in a plastic
cup, and poured
a bowl of dull

water, cleaned
of chlorine.
The temperature
of the surface
air, not
tampered with

by we
who fear
the murky,
love the cold.
If you don't
want to know

what resides
in the deepest
grass, don't
bring your eye
to the ground.
There once

was a man
who knew
how to read,
but didn't.
She emptied
the cup

into the bowl
and the fish
hid in a plastic
castle until
it was time to eat
his pinch of food.

Quarry (II)

Mineral constellations are glittering
beneath us. Rock is rock, an obstacle
in every direction. Our voices return to us
hollow from without, rocketing off
not bone and blood, but rock.

Incandescent floods are hung
from slightly slack wire, so the men
can work through evening, into night.
In their light the post-blast dust
is caught parachuting into the pit.

Let this be clear as if it were in sun.
They imagine the houses around them
in midday as they stop to eat: men
of incandescence, measuring time
by the unmined dome above.

The dome below is half exhausted,
bearing the marks of its value, mined
in the light, mined in the dark,
and only half exhausted. They will not live
to see it spent, what will fill the bare

earth, or what flat faulty place that keeps
their voices now will be hollowed,
pocked, a halved moon where other men
will leave our marks and hear a calling
from the other side: their own raised voices.

Ivan with Kerosene Lamp

He was a floating light,
hoove-like rustling at the root.
We turned from watching

the spot from which
the star fell. What should be
there now? Do limbs,

once gone, come back
to go again? We didn't speak,
but fixed our eyes on the last place

we heard him, believing
things freeze out of view.
What if it was wounded

and we stood there, dumb?
What if it saw a marbling
through us: our weakness,

our power, in the way
that we kept just to the edge
of the woods? That night,

we had stepped out to see
small lights falling
in a far black vastness

so that one drum beating
or not beating would seem,
for a second, nothing more

than what it was. The pain
we wake to is not ours
now, but the burning,

hurtling star's. We both
breathed in, aloud, and then
heard the dry leaves quieting.

We have seen people plant
rootless markers
in the place they were left,

so we will look and think
of them: a planter and one
of their dead. We stared

at the spot the star fell from—
Blank, Blank— but could not
set a stone there. A lantern

moving in the trees made us turn,
left us
with another sky to search

for light. We watched
the last place we saw it.
We might have heard singing.

We heard a hand raking
the floor of the woods
in search of something,

and this was the thing,
the place where it fell,
that had nothing to do with us.

Together, we felt
for give in the dark—
the path left by our heat—

and it carried us back. It will
not be covered. The sky will change.
It has nothing to do with us.

Notes

The Weekend Book is derived from the 1955 edition of the book of the same name (Nonesuch Press), a guide to the English countryside.

Alive Enough begins with a line by Thomas Hardy.

In *Not Fever, Not Dream,* the line *I've been where you most fear to be* is Robert Duncan.

Quarry (II) is a response to Wallace Stevens's *Evening with Angels.*

Ivan With Kerosene Lamp borrows from Sylvia Plath's *Nick and the Candlestick:* "The pain/You wake to is not yours."

Acknowledgments

Thank you to the editors of the journals where some of these poems appeared, some in a different form:

American Letters & Commentary, Blackbird, Boston Review, Cannibal, 42 Opus, Gut Cult, Little Red Leaves, Memorious, New American Writing, No Tell Motel, Octopus, Phoebe, Saint Elizabeth Street, Tarpaulin Sky, and *Typo.*

Portico appeared in the anthology *The Bedside Guide to the No Tell Motel* (No Tell Press, 2006)

Thank you to Jon Thompson for invaluable support, and to everyone at Parlor Press. Admiration and appreciation to Anita Huffington. Love and gratitude to Davis, Warren and Charlotte.

About the Author

Carolyn Guinzio is the author of one previous collection of poems, *West Pullman*, winner of the 2004 Bordighera Poetry Prize. A Chicago native, she received a BA from Columbia College and an MFA from Bard College. Her work has appeared in *Blackbird, Colorado Review, Denver Quarterly, 42 Opus, Indiana Review, New American Writing*, and many other journals. She has received awards from the arts councils of Kentucky and Illinois and now lives in Fayetteville, Arkansas.

Photograph of the author by Warren McCombs. Used by permission.

Free Verse Editions

Edited by Jon Thompson

2008

Quarry by Carolyn Guinzio
Between the Twilight and the Sky by Jennie Neighbors
The Prison Poems by Miguel Hernández,
    translated by Michael Smith
remanence by Boyer Rickel
What Stillness Illuminated by Yermiyahu Ahron Taub

2007

Child in the Road by Cindy Savett
Verge by Morgan Lucas Schuldt
The Flying House by Dawn-Michelle Baude

2006

Physis by Nicolas Pesque, translated by Cole Swensen
Puppet Wardrobe by Daniel Tiffany
These Beautiful Limits by Thomas Lisk
The Wash by Adam Clay

2005

A Map of Faring by Peter Riley
Signs Following by Ger Killeen
Winter Journey [Viaggio d'inverno] by Attilio Bertolucci,
    translated by Nicholas Benson

Printed in the United States
210576BV00001B/58-108/P